JAZZ MASTERS

Bud Powell

JAZZ MASTERS

Bud Powell

by Clifford Jay Safane

Amsco Publications
New York/London/Sydney

Book and cover design by Barbara Hoffman
Cover photo by David Gahr
Edited by Peter Pickow

Order No. AM 24316
International Standard Book Number: 0.8256.4082.2

Exclusive Distributors:
Music Sales Corporation
225 Park Avenue South, New York, NY 10003 USA
Music Sales Limited
8/9 Frith Street, London W1V 5TZ England
Music Sales Pty. Limited
120 Rothschild Street, Rosebery, Sydney, NSW 2018, Australia

Printed in the United States of America by
Vicks Lithograph and Printing Corporation

Contents

Bud Powell (1924-1966)

Earl "Bud" Powell was one of jazz's most influential pianists. Elements of his style can be heard in the playing of virtually all pianists of his own and later generations. A virtuoso improvisor, he played and recorded with many of the great musicians of his time, including Charlie Parker, Dizzy Gillespie, Sonny Stitt, and Dexter Gordon.

Born on September 27, 1924, in New York City, Powell was introduced to music at an early age. His grandfather, father, and brother William each played an instrument. (His younger brother, Richie, later became pianist with the Clifford Brown/Max Roach Quintet.) Bud began playing piano at the age of six, and continued his studies for the next seven years.

Powell's talent developed rapidly. He left school at fifteen to play in Coney Island clubs. He also started showing up at after-hours sessions in Harlem. It was during this time that Thelonious Monk befriended Powell, encouraging the young pianist to sit in at Minton's, where the new bebop style was being shaped.

Unfortunately, Powell's personal life was chaotic. At the age of twenty-one, he was arrested for disorderly conduct and then beaten; many feel that this treatment was a cause of his ensuing emotional problems. During the same year, the pianist made his first of many visits to a mental institution, receiving electroshock therapy and ammoniated water dousings. This probably adversely affected his creativity, but one can only speculate as to how different medical treatment might have influenced him.

The late 1940s and early 1950s were the most consistently creative years of Powell's career. By the mid 1950s, his personal problems had robbed his work of much of its vitality and technical brilliance. In 1959, he left New York for the less pressured atmosphere of Paris. His physical and mental health did improve somewhat, but he was never again his former self. His playing was erratic, although on occasion he played superbly.

Powell returned to New York in 1964, where he played Birdland and several other engagements. However, he was no longer the dynamic innovator that he had been at his peak. He died on August 1, 1966, of tuberculosis, alcoholism, and malnutrition.

Powell's style is characterized by a razor-sharp percussive touch, accenting his strong rhythmic thrust. On up-tempo material, he employs many lightning runs, giving his music an energy and excitement that few can duplicate. Single-note "horn-like" lines in the right hand are based on Charlie Parker's approach, although Powell transforms these elements into his own personal style. At the same time, the left hand plays a few spare chords which are sometimes dissonant in nature. This was unusual for the early 1940s when most pianists used an active left hand to maintain a basically steady rhythm. Since, in bebop, the drummer and bassist lay down the beat by themselves, Powell was free to use the left hand to accent the rhythm of his right-hand lines, as well as to mark the quickly-moving harmonic changes.

The following transcriptions of Powell's solos on "A Night in Tunisia" and "Tempus Fugit" show that his style is more than just a series of fast runs and accompanying chords. On "Tempus Fugit," Powell brilliantly creates a tension/release effect: He first increases the listener's expectation by repeating a rhythmic/melodic phrase, and then dissipates the growing tension by completing the unfinished musical thought.

Although the listener is usually first aware of Powell's rhythmic conception, a fine melodic sense is also evident. "Celia," for example, shows Powell's talent in this area. Even though the tempo is quick, he creates a series of connected flowing phrases that present a complete and satisfying musical thought.

It is on ballads, however, that Powell's lyricism (and a strong debt to Art Tatum) is most apparent. His textures now become thicker, with singing melodies supported by dense harmonies and moving inner voices. The pianist's romantic reading of "I'll Keep Loving You" showcases these characteristics. In addition, a personal rhythmic feel is also evident; Powell's elastic time-conception—employing both in-tempo and rubato passages—gives the music a breathing quality.

Despite his failing health and personal problems, Powell's artistic achievements were formidable. When one realizes that his creativity was expressed through improvisation, his accomplishments become even more impressive. He has left us a body of work that continues to influence pianists and move listeners.

Hallucinations

Earl "Bud" Powell
Transcribed and arranged by Clifford Jay Safane
Solo transcribed by Bob Himmelberger

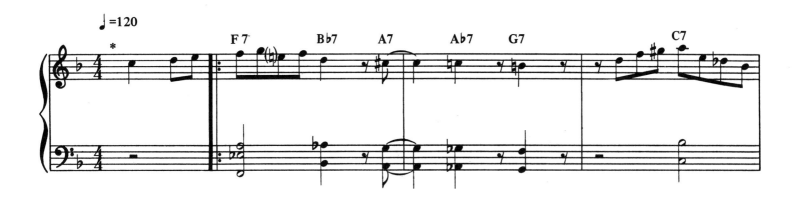

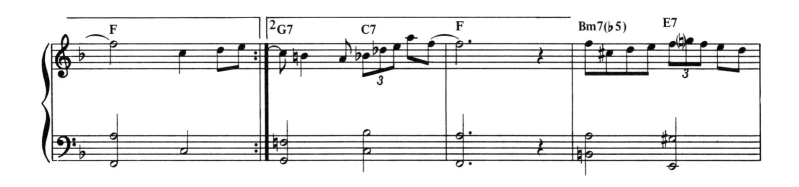

* In the following 32 bars (including the repeat), Powell plays the melody line an octave lower than what is written here.

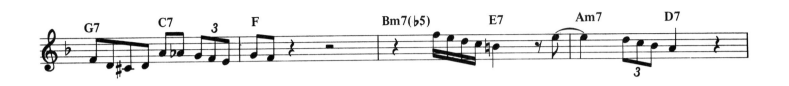

11

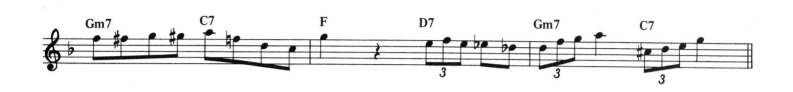

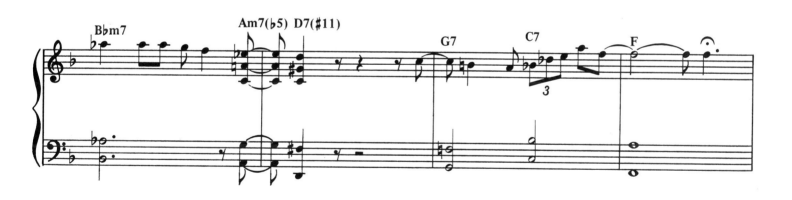

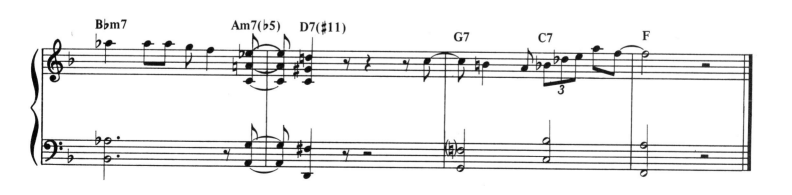

A Night In Tunisia

"Dizzy" Gillespie and Frank Paparelli
Solo transcribed by Bob Himmelberger

Strictly Confidential (Fool's Fancy)

Earl "Bud" Powell and Kenny Dorham
Transcribed and arranged by Clifford Jay Safane
Solo transcribed by Bob Himmelberger

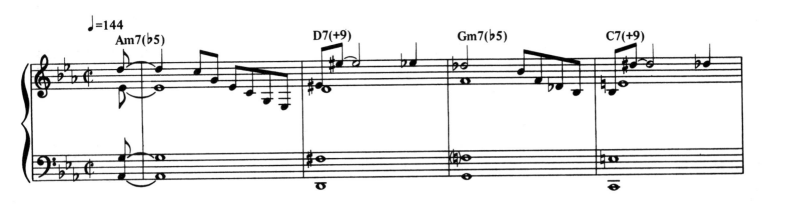

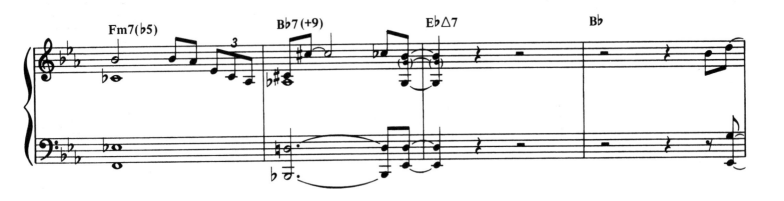

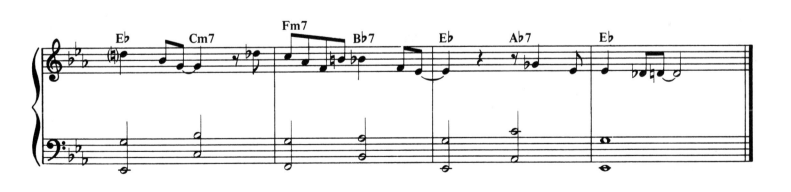

I'll Keep Loving You

Earl "Bud" Powell
Transcribed and arranged by Clifford Jay Safane

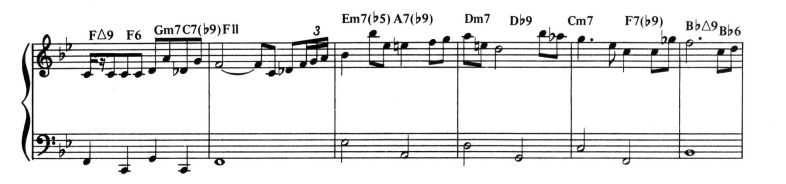

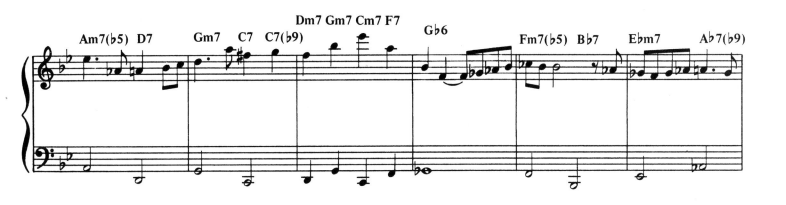

Tempus Fugit

Earl "Bud" Powell
Transcribed by Clifford Jay Safane
Solo transcribed by Jerry Kovarsky

*In the following 32 bars, Powell plays the melody line an octave lower than what is written here.

Celia

Earl "Bud" Powell
Transcribed and arranged by Clifford Jay Safane
Solo transcribed by Jerry Kovarsky

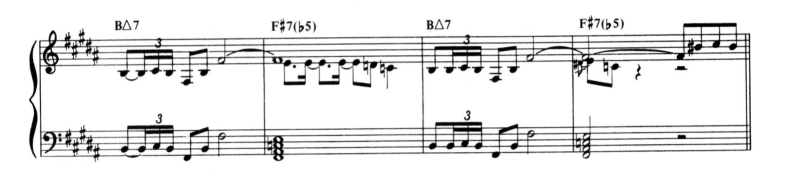

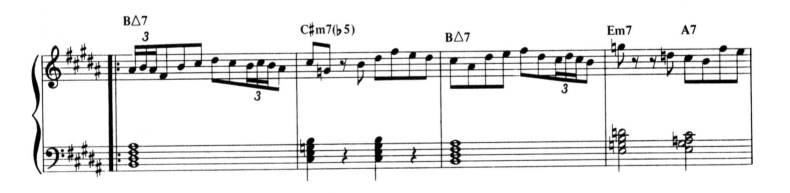

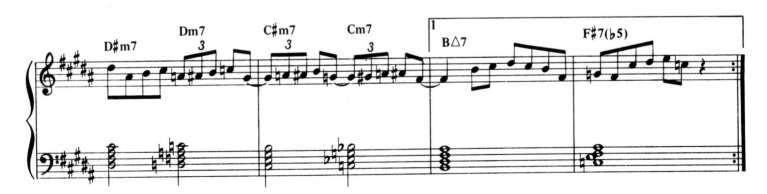

Discography

Bud Powell as Featured Artist

The Amazing Bud Powell, Volume 1 (includes "A Night in Tunisia")	Blue Note 81503
The Amazing Bud Powell, Volume 2	Blue Note 81504
Bud!, The Amazing Bud Powell, Volume 3	Blue Note 81571
Time Waits, The Amazing Bud Powell, Volume 4	Blue Note 81598
The Scene Changes, The Amazing Bud Powell, Volume 5	Blue Note 84009
The Genius of Bud Powell, Volume 1 (includes "Tempus Fugit," "Celia," "I'll Keep Loving You," "Strictly Confidential," and "Hallucinations")	Verve 2-2506
The Genius of Bud Powell, Volume 2	Verve 2-2526
"Strictly" Powell, Volume 1	RCA (Masters) 7193 (French import)
"Swingin' with Bud," Volume 2	RCA (Masters) 7312 (French import)
Essen Jazz Festival All Stars	Fantasy 86015
Bud Powell: 1924-66	ESP 1066
Ups 'n' Downs	Mainstream 385
Bud in Paris	Xanadu 102
A Portrait of Thelonious	Columbia 9092
The Best Years	Vogue 546 (French import)

Other recordings

Dexter Gordon, *Our Man in Paris*	Blue Note 84146
Fats Navarro, *Prime Source*	Blue Note 507-H2
Fat Girl	Savoy 2201
Charlie Parker, *One Night in Birdland*	Columbia 34808
Summit Meeting at Birdland	Columbia 34831
Bird—Savoy Recordings	Savoy 2201
Sonny Stitt, *Bud's Blues*	Prestige 7839
The Bebop Boys	Savoy 2225
The Greatest Jazz Concert Ever	Prestige 24024